Peter and the Wolf

Peter lives with his grandfather in a small village near a lake in a forest in Russia. In the winter it's very cold and it snows every day but in the spring the children go into the forest and play.

One sunny day Peter wants to play in the forest.
'You mustn't go there,' says Peter's grandfather.
'There are hungry wolves in the forest:
they're looking for food. They can't
find food under the snow!
When the snow melts,
you can play in the forest.'

Peter looks over the fence and sees Tweet, a little bird, talking to Quack, a duck.

The ice on the lake is melting and Quack is sitting in a pool of water.

'You're a stupid bird,' says Quack. 'You can't swim.'

'And you're a stupid bird because you can't sit in trees,' says Tweet.

Peter looks at the house. He can't see his grandfather.
'I'm not afraid of wolves,' he says to his cat, Theo.
He opens the gate and walks to the lake with Theo.

'Watch out, Tweet!' says Quack. 'Theo's coming and he wants to eat you!'
Tweet flies up onto a branch in the tree. Theo climbs up the tree onto another branch. They both look at Quack.
He tries to walk to Peter and… he slips… and slips… and slips on the ice!

Bump, bump, bump! Quack falls on the ice!
'Ouch!' says Quack. 'Ouch, ouch, ouch!'
Peter, Tweet and Theo laugh!
'You're a stupid bird,' says Tweet. 'You can't walk on the ice!'

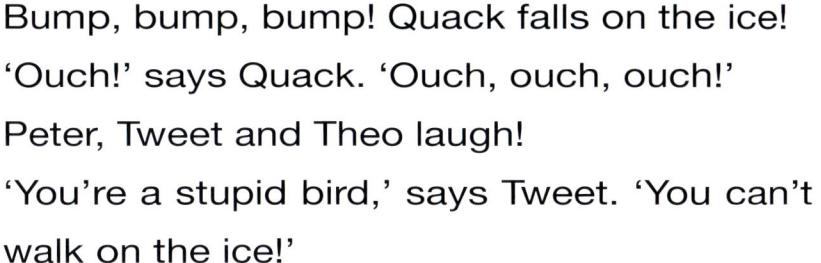

'Watch out!' shouts Tweet. 'The wolf's coming!'
The hungry wolf looks at Quack. He wants to eat him!
Quack slips and falls and slips and falls on the ice.
The wolf opens his mouth and tries to catch Quack.
Quack flies into the forest but the wolf runs after him!

Peter runs into the forest. He can't see the wolf but he can hear Quack.

'Help, help!' says Quack.

Peter sees the wolf… Oh no! The wolf's got feathers in his mouth!

Peter runs home
and finds a net.
He climbs up the tree.
The wolf sits under
the tree.
'I'm not afraid of the
wolf!' Peter says to
Tweet and Theo.
'And, I've got an idea…
Tweet, you can help
me catch the wolf!'

'You must fly down to the wolf and fly over his head and over his nose… up and down and round and round. Fly over his tail… up and down and round and round.
You must make the wolf dizzy!'

'I can't,' says Tweet. 'The wolf's hungry! He wants to eat me! I'm afraid!'

'You must fly UP when he opens his mouth,' says Theo. 'I know because birds always fly UP when I open my mouth and I NEVER catch a bird!'

The wolf looks up.
Tweet flies down.
She flies over the wolf's head and over the wolf's nose… up and down and round and round.
She flies over the wolf's tail… up and down and round and round!

The wolf runs round and round and round and round.
He's dizzy, he's very dizzy!
Bump! He falls down onto the snow!

Peter throws the net down over the wolf. He can't walk and he can't run!
'Wonderful!' says Theo.
'Yahoo!' shouts Quack.
'Look!' says Peter. 'It's Quack!… Quack! Are you OK?'
'I'm fine!' says Quack.
'I can't sit in trees or walk on the ice, but I can fly and… wolves can't catch me!

Peter's grandfather looks over the fence and sees Peter with Quack, Tweet and Theo.
He walks to the lake.
'Peter,' he says. 'What are you doing?'
'Look, Grandpa!' says Peter. 'We've got the wolf! Can we take him to the zoo?'

Peter's grandfather has an old lorry. He ties the net round the wolf and puts him onto the back of the lorry.

Peter, Quack, Tweet and Theo all sit in the front of the lorry with Peter's grandfather, and he drives them to the zoo.

When they arrive at the zoo, Peter's grandfather goes into the office.
Peter and his friends get out of the lorry.
They look at the wolf on the back of the lorry.
The wolf looks up at them.
'He's sad,' says Theo.
'He's very sad,' says Tweet.
'He doesn't want to live in the zoo,' says Quack.
'He wants to be free,' says Peter.

Peter looks at the wolf.

The wolf looks at Peter.

Peter climbs up onto the back of the lorry and unties the net.

The wolf jumps off the lorry.

'You're free now,' says Peter.
The wolf turns, looks at Peter and runs away into the forest.

Can you remember the story?

1 Look at the colours and make 5 sentences about the story.

1 Peter ……………………………………………………………………
2 Tweet ……………………………………………………………………
3 Quack ……………………………………………………………………
4 Theo ……………………………………………………………………
5 The wolf ……………………………………………………………………

What is the right word?

2 Choose the correct word.

in   on

1 The snow melts ...in... the spring.
2 Birds sit .... branches .... trees.
3 Quack slips .... the ice.
4 Peter, Quack, Tweet and Theo all sit .... the front of the lorry.

under   over

5 The wolf can't find food .... the snow.
6 Peter looks .... the fence.
7 The wolf sits .... the tree.
8 Tweet flies .... the wolf's head.

into   onto

9 In the spring the children go .... the forest and play.
10 Peter's grandfather puts the wolf .... the back of the lorry.
11 Peter's grandfather goes .... the office.
12 Peter climbs up .... the back of the lorry.

Yes or no?

3 **Look and read. Write yes or no answers.**

		Answer
1	Peter is looking at Quack.	Yes
2	Tweet is sitting on a branch in the tree.	....
3	Theo is sitting under the tree.	....
4	Peter is slipping on the ice.	....
5	Quack is trying to fly.	....
6	Quack is falling on the ice.	....
7	Peter, Tweet and Theo are laughing at Quack.	....
8	Tweet can't walk on the ice.	....

The fishing game

4 Help Peter, Tweet, Quack and Theo to catch words. There are two words on each fishing line.

Write the words.

1 Tweet ....in............... ....
2 Quack ....
3 Theo ....
4 Peter ....

Can you write a sentence with the words?

....

Picture crossword

5 Look at the pictures in the picture crossword. Write the first letter of each word in the correct box.

Example:
yellow = y

Put the words from the crossword in the correct sentence.

1 Tweet isn't a cat; she's a ....
2 The .... on the lake is melting.
3 Birds always .... up when Theo opens his mouth, and he never catches a bird!
4 Tweet flies up and down and round and round and makes the wolf ....

26 • ACTIVITIES

Draw and colour

6 Draw the characters and colour the picture.

- Draw Tweet. She's sitting on a branch.
- Draw the wolf. He's coming out of the forest.
- Draw Quack. He's slipping on the ice.
- Draw Peter. He's talking to Quack.
- Draw Theo. He's climbing up the tree.

Word puzzle

7 There are 50 words in the grid. Can you find them all?

S	A	S	H	O	U	S	E	I	C	W	I	N	T	E	R	I
P	D	T	U	B	S	H	O	U	T	R	E	E	Y	S	U	S
R	N	U	N	G	M	O	U	T	H	N	H	V	A	Q	S	L
I	E	P	G	R	A	N	D	F	A	T	H	E	R	U	S	I
N	T	I	R	O	L	I	V	E	P	A	E	R	O	S	I	P
G	H	D	Y	Z	L	O	O	K	C	L	L	R	U	U	A	J
A	R	F	E	A	T	H	E	R	A	K	P	E	N	N	T	N
T	O	U	C	H	B	U	M	P	T	F	O	Z	D	N	E	O
E	W	O	P	O	F	F	I	C	E	L	O	R	R	Y	K	S
S	O	A	W	O	N	D	E	R	F	U	L	S	H	O	M	E
W	L	A	U	G	H	V	Z	O	O	L	A	F	R	A	I	D
I	F	G	A	N	O	T	H	E	R	U	K	T	O	D	C	R
M	E	L	T	A	I	L	W	I	E	F	E	N	C	E	E	I
O	I	D	E	A	N	K	E	M	S	N	O	W	L	A	E	V
U	B	I	R	D	U	C	K	X	T	H	R	O	W	T	F	E

How many words can you find?

50 – Excellent
35 – 45 Very good
25 – 35 Good
10 – 25 Quite good

Picture Dictionary

wolf (wolves)

cat

duck

bird

feather

nose

head

mouth

tail

lake

pool

water

forest

tree

branch

village

house

zoo

office

fence

gate

lorry

snow	fall
ice	throw
melt	catch
winter	run
spring	fly
afraid	drive
sad	laugh
jump	shout
climb	talk
walk	tie
slip	untie

eat

in

on

under

over

into

onto

Key

Activity 1:
1 Peter lives with his grandfather.
2 Quack slips on the ice.
3 Tweet must make the wolf dizzy.
4 Theo never catches a bird.
5 The wolf doesn't want to live in the zoo.

Activity 2:
1 in, 2 on, 3 on, 4 in, 5 under, 6 over, 7 under, 8 over, 9 into, 10 onto, 11 into, 12 onto.

Activity 3:
1 yes, 2 yes, 3 no, 4 no, 5 no, 6 yes, 7 yes, 8 no

Activity 4:
Tweet: in, Russia
Quack: small, village
Theo: Peter, lives
Peter: in, a
Peter lives in a small village in Russia.

Activity 5:

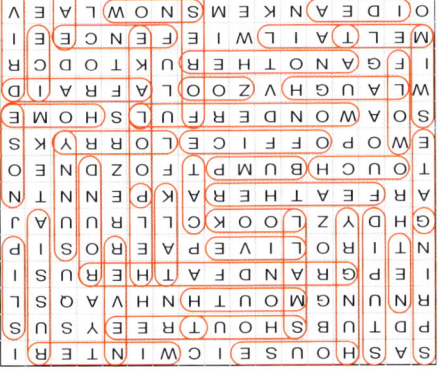

Activity 6:
Open answers

Activity 7:

afraid, another, bird, bump, cat, drive, duck, eat, feather, fence, forest, gate, grandfather, help, home, house, hungry, ice, idea, lake, laugh, live, look, lorry, melt, mouth, net, never, nose, office, ouch, pool, round, Russia, shout, slip, small, snow, spring, stupid, sunny, swim, tail, talk, throw, tree, winter, wolf, wonderful, zoo

ACTIVITIES • 31

Editor: Robert Hill
Design and art direction: Nadia Maestri
Computer graphics: Simona Corniola

© 2011 Black Cat

First edition: January 2011

DEALINK, DEAFLIX are trademarks licensed by
De Agostini SpA

All rights reserved. No part of this book may be reproduced, stored in a retrieval system, or transmitted, in any form or by any means, electronic, mechanical, photocopying, recording or otherwise, without the written permission of the publisher.

We would be happy to receive your comments and suggestions, and give you any other information concerning our material.
info@blackcat-cideb.com
blackcat-cideb.com

The Publisher is certified by
CISQCERT
in compliance with the UNI EN ISO 9001:2008 standards for the activities of «Design and production of educational materials» (certificate no. 02.565)

Printed in Italy by Litoprint, Genoa